WRITE LEFT

WRITE LEFT

Sujaya Devi

8-2019

Seeta,
Thank you for re-connecting
with the family after so
many years. I appreciate
your support of
my book!

Life Rattle Press, Toronto

—Sujaya

Write Left

Life Rattle Press, Toronto, Canada
Copyright © 2017 by Sujaya Devi
All Rights Reserved.

ISBN 978-1-987936-48-3

Typeset and Cover Design by Sujaya Devi
Edited by Lyndsay Sinko

For my Nana

What a strange world.

— Douglas Coupland

Contents

Epilogue:

Chapter 1: Write Left

We remember the things we learn from scratch.

Today, I'm Cinderella. I slide the pair of princess shoes from the busted box. Unlike Cinderella's glass shoes, mine are plastic. I slide both feet through the carpet to the top step.

Time for my grand entrance.

My foot misses the step. As my shoe falls off, I tumble down the stairs. I somersault until my head smacks against the wall. I sit up. Mom stands beside me. She holds my heels and looks at me with a half-grin.

"I'm okay," I announce. I stand and pull up the poof of my blue dress.

"What happened?" Mom asks in a hushed voice.

"I slipped."

I wipe blood from my knee with my hand, careful not to let it touch my princess dress.

"Sit here." Mom steps away and comes back from the kitchen with a small white square, Polysporin, and a Band-Aid. Mom places a pink Band-Aid over the scrape. "All clean."

I hold my shoes up towards the light. "Do you like them?" I wiggle them in the air to make the glitter sparkle.

Mom laughs. "That's why you fell?" She smooths my tangled hair.

I pass my finger over the pink Band-Aid. "Yeah . . ."

"Be careful with those. You could sprain your ankle when you wear heels," Mom explains.

"Okay," I say. "Want to see the other ones?" I ask.

"Sure. Be careful walking down the stairs and hold the rail this time," Mom says, hitting her hand against the rail.

I lift the poof of my dress again and scurry up the stairs, barefoot. This time, I grab the white pair of princess shoes from the box and jump into them. I tiptoe to the stairs, step forward, slip, and roll.

"Ouchie."

My brother Saikiran giggles as he runs over to the stairs. Teenage Mutant Ninja Turtles plays in the living room. "What did you do?" he asks.

"My shoe fell off." My elbow feels tender. My hand stings.

Mom turns off the stove and walks over. "You didn't hold the rai—."

"—I tried to catch my shoe," I explain.

My great-grandfather—we call him Poy— whistles softly as he puts cans of condensed and evaporated milk in the fridge. Poy stirs his tea beside the stove. He glances at the three of us hovering around the stairs. He covers his tea with a saucer and closes the cupboard. He stops whistling when he sees my bandaged knee and arm.

"W'happen to she?"

"She fell dong de stairs," Mom says with a Trini accent.

I use my foot to drag the princess shoes in front of me. I put them back on.

Poy looks back and forth at the shoes on my feet.

"Cha-leen, she shoes wrongside," he says.

"Huh?" I ask.

"Go an' sit outside. I go show yuh."

I take my fold-out stool from the living room to the backyard and wait on the deck. Poy balances a Sharpie on my box of princess shoes as he walks outside.

"Lehme show yuh someting," Poy says. He pulls a sun-bleached deck chair beside me. "Hold out yuh han' like this." He points with one finger and his thumb. I point with one finger and my thumb. "Dis shape is an 'L.' Match dis shape wit dis shoe." He draws the mark on one shoe. "Dis is de left heel."

He picks up the other shoe. He draws another line.

"Dis is the right-side shoe." He hands both marked shoes to me. He picks out another pair of princess shoes. He re-draws the marks on those shoes.

He hands me the shoe with the pointy mark. "What yuh call dis shoe?"

"The left shoe?" I guess.

"Good." Poy points back and forth, back and forth between my feet. He stops. "Which foot is de left foot?"

I point my "L" down at the foot beneath it.

"Good. Which foot is de right foot?" he quizzes.

I point at the other foot.

"Good. Now, you cyah wear yuh shoes wrong-side." Poy lines up my shoes ahead of me, pair by pair. "Here." He uncaps the jumbo Sharpie and holds the cover. I wrap my hand around the marker.

"What do I do?" I ask.

Poy takes the marker from my hand. He places the marker on my middle finger and forms a pinch with my first finger and thumb. He hands me a princess shoe. "Write left."

CHAPTER 2: WRONG INGREDIENTS

We get lost and find ourselves.

Y ou guys hungry? I can make a bread-
cheese-soya for you," Lini Mami says.
"Who said bread-cheese-soya?" my cousin
Anand asks as he walks in from the backyard.
"You guys should try it. It's bread, cheese, and
soya. I invented a sandwich, or Mom calls it a
sangwich."

"I'm good," I answer.

"Me too," Saikiran says.

"I goin' to do some laundry upstairs. Tell me if
de boys bugging you, okay Jaya?"

"Okay."

Saikiran and I stand in the living room beside
the tangled Nintendo 64 controllers. Adithya shouts
something from outside. His voice gets louder.
"Anand! Anaaand! Where did it go?" Adithya runs
inside holding a small crystal glass. "Anand!" He
stops running when he sees Saikiran and I. Adithya
holds his hand out for a fist-bump. "Wazza Kirz?
Wazza Jaya?"

"Did you guys see Spiderman?" Anand asks.

"Yeah," Saikiran and I say in sync.

Anand swirls the grey liquid around in the glass.

"Do you want powers too?" Adithya asks.

"Dunno," I say.

"Ya . . . I dunno," Saikiran agrees.

Anand holds the glass up to our eyes. The glass is filled with some kind of oil that floats above another liquid and brown lumps at the bottom. I flinch.

"We're making a potion," he says.

"We're gonna be like Spiderman," Adithya says. He takes the glass from Anand and swishes around the stuff inside.

"We even found a spider to use," Anand says. "Let's go catch it before it runs away."

We mission to the backyard. Adithya and Anand scan the wall brick by brick. A tiny ball with eight legs dangles above their heads.

"I don't see it," Adithya says.

"Come on you idiot, it's right there!" Anand shouts.

"Shut up six year old! I couldn't see it with your big ears in the way. Respect your elders." Adithya hands Anand the potion glass and picks up newspapers from the pile in the sandbox. Adithya holds the newspaper beneath the spider as it climbs onto the page. Adithya folds the page and flattens the spider. He scrapes the spider-guts and adds them to the potion. "*This* is what you need to get your spidey powers."

"I don't thi—" I start.

"Guys! We forgot to add milk!" Anand interrupts. He rushes to the kitchen. "Milk makes you strong," he says, pouring milk drops in the glass. He rests the milk jug on the counter.

"Milk is gross if you think about it," I say. "Did you know it comes from a cow?"

Anand shrugs. "What else did we forget to add?" he asks.

Saikiran shrugs. "You sure you wanna drink that?"

Anand nods. "I want powers."

"That looks dirty," I add.

Saikiran nods.

"We can clean it with soap," Anand says. He turns to the sink and pumps purple dish soap to the mix. Anand holds the glass near mine and Saikiran's and faces.

"Ugh. That smells weird," I say pulling my t-shirt to cover my nose.

Saikiran nods.

"I know how to make it smell good," Adithya says. He runs from the kitchen to the basement stairs and disappears. He reappears with a bottle of brown liquid. "It needs musk," he says spritzing the spider potion with a dose of perfume.

"How do you make it look good?" I ask staring at the cloudy mixture.

"We can find something downstairs," Adithya says and jets to the stairs. We run behind him.

In the basement I find a vial of glitter among bins of Power Ranger action figures, Pokémon figures, G.I. Joes, and Lego pieces. "What about this?" I joke.

"Good idea," Adithya says. He pinches specks of silver dust and sprinkles them into the glass.

"You guys ready to drink it?" he asks.

"No thanks. Not me," I answer.

Saikiran shakes his head. "Nah, I'm okay."

"You're losing out on the spidey senses," Adithya says. "Alright, Anand. We can split this."

"Here." I hand Anand a bottle of water from the case in the corner. "You might need this."

"You first, Anand," Adithya says. He hands Anand the glass.

"No, you first," Anand says and pushes the glass back.

"Fine. I'm ready for my spidey senses," Adithya says. Saikiran covers his eyes.

Adithya slurps down half of the dirty musk water. His nose wrinkles and his eyes water. Adithya gags. Saikiran gags. Anand gags. I gag.

I'm glad I didn't eat the bread-cheese-soya.

He coughs as Anand opens the bottle of water for him to chug.

"My turn," Anand says. He downs the rest of the musk water like he would a glass of milk. Anand puts a hand over his mouth and hunches over.

Footsteps creek from above us.

"Adithya! Anand! Who leave out de milk?!"

CHAPTER 3: SCRIBBLES

Sathya is the word for truth. Speak the truth.

I throw my knapsack into a cubby before I hug Mom goodbye. Strangers fill the room. Strangers spread out between the play space, the book baskets, the easels, and the water table. The other moms stand beside the stainless steel sink and talk about how tanned they got this summer. They look pale to me.

"Hi Sujaya! How nice to see you. Ready for your first day?" Mrs. Maclean asks. The first time I met Mrs. Maclean was last year when Saikiran started kindergarten at Sawmill Valley. Her silver-framed glasses brighten her grey eyes. Her fair skin peeks through the Velcro straps of her sandals.

"Yeah," I say.

The moms haven't moved. One mom has red lipstick on her collar and red lipstick covers the lid of her white coffee cup. Another has blonde-but-almost-white hair. She spins her rhinestone keychain around her finger. The other mom nods along as they compare their high heeled shoes. This mom looks like she was dipped in sequins. Her shoes and shirt are stitched with sequin flowers.

Boys pour bins of giant Lego and wooden blocks on the floor of the front room by the rocking chair. Girls braid each other's hair around the Beanie babies bin. I visit the art table. Stacked bins of pencil crayons, Crayola markers, and rulers cover it. I grab the marker bin and construction paper. I arrange the markers in order of the rainbow from red to violet. I scribble with each colour to fill the page. I draw a sunny sky, a beach, and palm trees. On another page, I draw Mom and her red Accord beside me at Sawmill Valley Public School.

The moms watch me draw. They're talking about summer at the cottage. *Is that where they make the cheese?* The lady with red lipstick on her collar walks up to me. I cap the red marker.

"What's your name?" she asks.

"Sujaya," I say, drawing a window.

"Sujaya . . . That's an . . . interesting name," she says. She pulls a strand of light brown hair away from her eyes as she crouches to talk to me. The girls by the Beanie babies have the same light brown hair.

"Yeah," I say.

"Why don't you go make some friends?" she asks. A bit of gold shines on her front tooth as she speaks.

I uncap a black marker and fill in the window

frame. "I have friends."

Sequin lady walks up to us. "You can make new friends," she says.

"Why?" I ask. I switch the black marker for a blue one.

She stops. "You can play with the other girls," sequin lady says.

I ignore her. I switch back to the black marker. I take a sheet of pink construction paper and draw a black cloud. I use the blue marker to draw rain. The blonde lady's heels click as she walks over to us. I put the markers back in the bin and pick up my drawings. A girl sits at the other end of the table drawing by herself. I walk over to her. The moms smile at me.

"Want to be friends?" I ask. Sequin lady gives me a thumbs-up.

"Sure," the girl answers. She looks a lot like sequin lady, brownish-red hair, light brown eyes, and a sequined shirt. "What's your name?"

"I'm Sujaya. What's yours?"

"That's a cool name. I'm Cora."

Blonde-but-almost-white haired lady calls a blonde-but-almost-white haired girl over to us. "Sujaya, this is Peggy."

I wave. "Hi, Peggy."

The moms smile at me as they walk over to Mrs. Maclean to say goodbye. Peggy's friends walk over to the table. The girls ask Cora if she wants them

17

to braid her hair. They all have the same braids, some are blonde and some are light brown. "Do you want to come too?" Cora asks. She points to the rug where Peggy and the other girls sat with the Beanie Babies.

Two easels sit beside the art table across the room. I watch as the girls line up Beanie babies on the rug. A drawer beside the easels has paint brushes, paint trays, and paint.

"I'm okay," I say. "I'd rather paint."

CHAPTER 4: PAPER FLAMES

Thanks, Mom.

Wind up the wine-dow," Mom says. She eases the car to a full stop. "I'll pick you up at three. Is that good?"

I wind the handle and the window closes. "Mhmm," I say as I unbuckle my seatbelt.

"Have fun with Margaret," Mom adds.

"Okay, see you later," I say and close my door. I wave bye to Mom as she drives off.

Margaret and I became friends a year ago in third grade. I don't remember how we became friends, but I think it involved popsicle sticks.

Tufts of moss grow between the interlocking bricks of Margaret's driveway. A bare blackberry tree stands beside it. A bristly mat in front of the door has an inky outline of a cat and a dog sitting beside the word "WELCOME." It's the kind of mat people hide keys under. The thin window panel beside the door is covered in stickers, stained-glass art, and a sign that reads, "Our dog is friendly." I press the star-stickered doorbell. Chimes sound, followed by gallops moving towards the door.

"I'll get it!" The shout sounds like Margaret, but it might be her sister, Maddie. They have similar squeaky voices. The door swings open. Margaret has a string of multi-coloured beads around her neck, orange paint on her jeans, and glitter glue smudged on her cheek. "Hi Sujaya! Come on in," she squeals.

I step inside and untie my shoes.

"Oh, you don't have to take off your shoes. We keep our shoes on inside the house," Margaret explains.

"Oh. Okay," I say, looping and knotting my shoelaces.

"I set out some art supplies in the kitchen for us. I'll show you," Margaret says. She leads me to the kitchen. A paper plate hangs on the wall. The plate, covered in cat stickers, hangs from a purple ribbon. Photos of Margaret and Maddie are framed around it. "Right now it's an art room," she says. This week's No-Frills flyer is scattered across the table, covered in pipe-cleaners, paint, and popsicle sticks. "Wait. I forgot. I have something for you! You can sit. I'll be back!" Sometimes Margaret reminds me of my kindergarten teacher, Mrs. Maclean. Mrs. Maclean used to speak like that.

Margaret dashes through the kitchen, runs up and back down the stairs, then slides back into the kitchen and over to me. "Here." Margaret hands me an egg carton with hot-glued pieces of red, orange, and yellow construction paper. The pieces of paper are layered in the shape of a tea tree leaf. Each egg compartment holds one red-orange-yellow leaf. "I made this for you," Margaret says.

I hesitate. "Cool . . ." I say.

"These are divas. Happy Diwali!" She beams.

"A wha—?" On second glance, they aren't leaves, they're flames. "A diya?" I ask.

"You're Hindi, right? I heard that it was Diwali soon and I wanted to make you something. These are divas, the little lamps Hindis set up when they celebrate."

"Oooh. Um . . . Yeah, I am *Hindu*. Diwali is next week," I explain.

"Did you know that Diwali is the festival of lights?" Margaret asks.

"Ye—" an alarm on the oven beeps twice at a time.

"Moooooooooom! The scones are ready!" Margaret screeches.

"Coming, Margaret!" Margaret's mom yells from the top step. She speeds down the stairs to take out a tray of little bread buns. "These scones look scrumptious if I do say so myself," Margaret's mom says.

Margaret catches me staring at the tray of puffed, patty-shaped bread. "It's like a flaky bread."

"Cool," I say.

"Hindis eat naan bread, right?" Margaret's mom asks.

"Some *Hindus* do. They just call it naan. It's kind of like saying scone bread . . . you just say naan," I say.

"I find that really interesting," Margaret says. "I think we bought some naan bread at that little Indian place, right Mom?"

"That's right Margaret. They made it in that little oven," Margaret's mom says. She holds the tray of scones with a triple-folded bread cloth and places it on the stove.

"Trini people make roti, though. It's another type of bread," I explain. Margaret and her mom don't respond. Margaret pours glue on a paper saucer.

"Alright girls, I'll get out of your way," Margaret's mom says. She grooves her way out of the kitchen.

"Margaret, what else do you know about Diwali?" I ask.

"Hindis pray like this," she says. She stands up. She places her hands together, lifts her elbows, and bows.

"That's what we do," I jest.

"I know," Margaret says. "Let's finish these popsicle card holders before your mom comes back." Margaret lines up popsicle sticks and places strips of masking tape over them to make squares.

I mimic her steps. We listen to CHFI radio and

the SleepCountry jingle gets stuck in my head. I don't know any of the songs. I peel dried glitter glue from my hands like a weird extra layer of skin.

*

The doorbell chimes. Margaret and I peek through the kitchen to see who it is.

"Oh, hello, Charlene!" Margaret's mom announces. Margaret and I tidy up and wash our hands, pick up our card holders, divas, and head to the door.

Mom raises an eyebrow when she sees the egg carton in my hand. I raise my shoulders and eyebrows too.

"Happy Diwali," Margaret says. "I made divas for you guys. Sujaya said you guys were Hindi."

"That's very nice. We are *Hindu*. Thank you, Margaret," Mom says.

"Speaking of Hindi," Margaret's mom says, "How's Vishnu?"

Mom looks at me. I give her wide eyes.

"Sorry?" Mom asks.

"Yes. Vishnu? The god or something?" Margaret's mom says. Margaret stands behind her mom counting the beads on her necklace.

I wait for Mom's response.

"Oh, Vishnu. He's fine," Mom says.

I'm relieved. Margaret's mom looks humoured. Mom exhales. "How's Jesus?"

My eyes widen.

Margaret's mom chuckles.

Mom puts her hand on my shoulder and squeezes. "We should get going," she says. "Thanks for the divas, Margaret."

CHAPTER 5: LEVEL TWO

We download an update.

1 36-A is the strangest classroom at Erindale. It has two levels. Level One has a balcony-like storage space for broken monitors, circuit boards, and extension cables. Level Two has a play space for the technologically inclined. I've entered Level Two, the classroom. I pretend that the drills, clamps, and power saws don't intimidate me. In the far right corner is a control panel of knobs, switches, and buttons. A big red button stands out. The sign reads: "DO NOT TOUCH."

My grade eleven girl-friends are in food and nutrition, yet here I am.

I know a few guys in this class, like Jason Runzer, Paul Bingham, and Andrew Block from Homeland's Middle School, but not well enough to join in their conversation about street hockey on Saturday. Level Two fills up with characters: the Local Area Network, or LAN, party gamers, the sci-fi kids, the country-loving jocks, and future computer scientists.

We grab wobbly stools and the guys surround Mr. Anderson's desk. I sit outside of the huddle. Mr. Anderson skitters into the room with attendance lists. He's another character, animated and excited to teach. He's younger than the majority of teachers I've had at Erindale this far. Mr. Anderson is young, probably young enough to get ID'd at a bar. He places attendance sheets on his desk.

Mr. Anderson steps ahead of the class and looks around. His eyes show surprise when he notices me. "Ladies and gentlemen, welcome." Mr. Anderson extends his arms to present the classroom. The attendance papers in his hands flutter as he motions around the room. He looks at me, at the guys huddled around him, then back at me. "I should say lady and gentlemen, welcome," he snickers. Mr. Anderson raises the attendance list and calls names. As he moves along the list he pauses. All murmurs turn to silence. "Sujaya, I'm looking at my attendance and you're the only girl in this class."

All eyes dart towards me.

I avoid direct eye contact with everyone in the room. "Yeah . . ." I say. I watch the Peel District School Board screensaver bounce from corner to corner on the screen behind Mr. Anderson's desk.

"Guys, you know what this means," he pauses. "You have to be nice to her. You aren't allowed to scare away the only girl in the class."

★

30

We're cruising through Lego Mindstorms and playing with robots, a typical day in TEJ3M0. Our goal today is to create programs that detect colours and distances so that the robot navigates through a maze in one go. The robot also must detect yellow, at which point it has to turn ninety degrees and push a water bottle out of the way. Once the bottle is moved, the robot has to return to the course. This maze occupies the central workspace of level two. It's four times my size. It's framed with white wooden panels. The robot's route is mapped out with coloured tape: a black track, yellow turning points, and a red finish line.

I connect the robot to my computer and transfer my program: "SUJAYA 1." The robot, made of Lego, ultrasonic, and colour sensors, and the brick (also known as the heart of the robot), reminds me of a puppy. It just swerves around, confused and imbalanced, wiggles and runs into walls. It doesn't know how to be a robot and it's our task to teach it. I feel like a mom.

I wait beside Paul and Jason as Andrew positions the robot at the starting line. It waddles along the black line then revs into the wall repeatedly.

"Nice one, Andrew," Paul says.

"Shut up, Paul," Andrew responds with a death stare. Jason chuckles.

Paul switches the program from "ANDREW 1" to "PAUL 1." He hits the grey square for the robot to start. The robot, I call him Proto, swings its back wheels left and right as it follows the black line of tape. Proto makes a sharp turn when it detects a wall ahead of it. As Proto turns, it switches directions, and heads back to start. The colour sensor detects red from the starting line. Proto does a 360 and powers down.

"Ha. Nice one, Paul!" Andrew shouts from his computer.

"Like yours was better," Paul taunts.

Jason takes Proto back to the starting line. "JASON 1," he presses the grey square. Proto moves full speed into the wall.

"Nice," Jason says. He lifts Proto and ends the program. "Here." He places Proto in my hands.

"Thanks." I hover down to "SUJAYA 1," and press the grey square. Proto charges full speed towards the first wall. Proto decides to play Ring Around the Rosie instead of turning at the corner. I sigh. I power Proto down and place him back at the starting line for the next hopeful participant.

I scoot back to my computer to adjust my program. I don't know where to start.

"Guys, remember that rotations means the number of times the tires will turn. If you want the robot to turn one way or the other, you need a fraction of a rotation on one side. But when in doubt, switch to degrees," Mr. Anderson announces.

I take Mr. Anderson's advice and play with degrees. I gamble with forty-five and ninety degree angles in my program instead of using tire rotations. I borrow Proto to download version two. "SUJAYA 2," saving, connecting, downloading, done. I rejoin the line. Test after test, we see the same things: Proto crashes into the wall, Proto turns and shuts down, Proto detects yellow and goes berserk.

Proto needs help.

Proto is back in my hands. Grey button. Go.

Proto wiggles its way down the black line swinging its hips. The way Proto swerves makes it look like one sassy robot. Wall detected, swerve.

"Hey, that's pretty good!" Mr. Anderson says walking towards the maze.

Proto wiggles down the second line. Swerve, swerve, swerve. *That's my baby.* Proto detects yellow, pauses, and turns. Proto rams into the water bottle and moves it. Proto turns back to the track and continues down the black taped path. Proto develops a pattern: detect yellow, pause, turn, push the bottle, pause, turn back, wiggle down the track.

"Wait. You did it!" Mr. Anderson shouts. "This is why we need more women in technology." He points at Proto stopped beside the knocked over water bottle. Mr. Anderson turns to the guys waiting in line to test their programs. "Did you see that? Did you?" He turns back to me, frenzied. "I said it on the first day and I'm glad you didn't drop this class. You're smarter than us." Mr. Anderson lifts

Proto like a trophy. "She figured it out! Be nice to her, she might help you." He laughs and turns to me. "I would just tweak it so that it doesn't swerve so much while it drives. It looks kinda sassy." He places Proto back on the track.

"I noticed that too," I say, laughing.

"You're on the right track. Literally."

"Thank you," I say.

"You're welcome. Sujaya, don't ever let boys intimidate you," Mr. Anderson says. "You're smarter than them."

CHAPTER 6: YELLOW

Some people's responses are so dry.
But don't worry homie, I got a humidifier.

Dark smudges surround her eyes. She sobs to the girl beside her at the sink. She holds a wad of toilet paper stained with mascara. I consider going back to the dining hall and using Mom's hand sanitizer after all. Instead, I hesitate as I approach the single bathroom sink to wash my hands.

"I asked for caramel." She uses the toilet paper to wipe her tears and runny makeup. Her peony pink lipstick shines against her warm honey skin tone.

"It's okay, really!" Her friend assures. Her friend's hair is pin straight with blonde streaks between her dark brown hair. "You look pretty!"

Her swollen eyes stare at her reflection in the soap-stained mirror. "I didn't think it would turn yellow! I asked for caramel." She holds a strand of bleached hair before her eyes. "This is yellow! How am I supposed to see these people with this yellow—?" Her screeches turn to sobs. She takes another wad of toilet paper from her straight-haired friend.

I close the tap.

"Doesn't her hair look nice?" the straight-haired girl asks.

I look back at Caramel. Her breath is shallow. Her hair is the same shade as Mr. Goudas' brand curry powder.

I picture myself with yellow hair. My family would roast me like they roast eggplant over a fire for bhaigan choka. "I don't think it looks yellow," I lie. "It looks nice." I chime.

She fixes on her reflection. "Really?" She wipes her eyes clean with the back of her dress sleeve.

"Seriously!" Her friend insists.

"Of course!" I echo.

She smiles. "I didn't want everyone to see me like this." She laughs.

"With your skin-tone you could pull off any colour," I respond. I throw my paper towel in the trash bin near the door.

She dabs around her eyes with toilet paper once more. She re-lines her swollen eyelids with a black pencil.

I return to the family dinner. Our gang of Trinidadians and Trinidadian-Canadians occupies the twenty-seater table. Uncle Jai and Aunty Zalina joke about the "*fohk* and knife." Fried rice, tofu, and wontons are already dished out for me. No roti tonight.

"What took you so long?" Mom asks.

I deliberate. "She wanted caramel, but she got yellow."

"What was yellow?" Mom looks at the bathroom sign and squints at me. She points to the fried rice on my plate. "Actually . . . just eat, I don't want to know."

CHAPTER 7: HIDE AND DON'T SEEK

Unlike Ontario, I'm not yours to discover.

Day 1: Almost 9:00AM

The waxed floors and fresh blackboards in IB 120 welcome the future class of 2017. The rows of seats in this lecture hall look endless. Two keeners sit in the front row, but the lecture hall is otherwise empty. During orientation, UTMSU, my students' union, was kind enough to give me a padfolio to write in. This padfiolio is a hybrid between a clipboard and a folder. I play with the latch and spring and watch the clasp secure my blank pages.

It's now five minutes to nine.

Squads assemble. Rows of coder boys line up their massive laptops that glow on the desk space that stretches across the row. A few other girls have already taken their seats. I count eight girls in total, including myself. Three of them jumped straight out of an anime convention, or so it seems, with their sailor skirts, striped knee highs, and fingerless gloves. They place their Asus laptops side-by-side, comparing schedules. The other four form another squad. They seem normal.

I try to look busy by writing the date on the top-right corner of the page.

"Is anyone sitting here?" a guy asks. His cellphone sits in his shirt pocket and the buttons are fastened all the way up. The legs of his jeans are folded at the bottom. He glances at my backpack on the seat beside me.

I look at the empty rows ahead, behind, and beside me. "No?" I say.

He waits. I wait. He looks at the seat.

I move my backpack.

He places his jacket on the seat and calls over his friends. Three guys walk over comparing cellphones. They do the high-five-fist-bump-hug thing. He calls over more of his friends and they do the high-five-fist-bump-hug thing. They place their Asus, Acer, and Lenovo laptops on the desk in that order. I rethink this padfolio.

My row is now full.

The guy beside me turns around and nods at the group of guys behind us. They fill the row. There are twenty-two other rows they could have chosen. I avoid eye contact. *Maybe I should move.*

"This is CSC108, right?" the guy asks.

"Yup. This is computer science," I say.

"I hear it's with Dan. He's supposed to be cool.

Are you in first year, too?" he asks.

"Yup."

"I'm Daron," he says.

"Hi," I say.

"What's your name?" he asks.

"Sujaya," I say.

"It's nice to meet you, Sujaya," he says.

"Yeah. You too."

"It's so rare to find a girl in computer science," Daron says.

"Yeah." I catch myself spinning my pen.

"I hope you don't mind, but my friends joined us." He points at the group of guys that now fill the row ahead of us, the row we sit in, and the row behind us. "They're a little intimidated because you're pretty and a girl." A young man with a red, black, and white cane walks to the podium.

"That's okay," I say. The young man rests his cane against the podium. I press the home button on my Blackberry. "9:08."

"So, what other courses are you taking?" Daron asks.

To my right, his friends grin at us. "I can't remember," I say. "I'm taking calculus for sure."

"Is that your schedule?" he points at the colour-coded schedule sticking out of my padfolio.

"Yeah . . . It is," I say. I slide my schedule on the desk.

"Nice. I'm in the same calculus and proofs lectures as you."

"You guys know each other?" another guy asks.

"We just met," Daron says. "This is Sujaya. Sujaya this is Haider." The two guys beside Haider smile and wave. "That's Hassan and that's Abid."

"Hi," I say.

"Girls never take computer science. It's so rare," Hassan says.

"Yeah," I respond.

"Usually girls go into life science or sociology," Abid says.

"That wasn't for me." The guys around us observe our interaction like they've never seen a conversation before.

"What else did you take?" Daron asks. His crew waits for an answer.

"I took communications tech, tech engineering, and tech design." Their eyebrows raise. They study me. I side-eye them. They look away.

"How was that?" Abid asks. He slouches back in his chair.

"It was awkward because I was the only girl in my tech class for two years." I sigh. Beyond this section of the lecture hall, girls smile as they chat—at ease.

"What? Too many guys creeping on you?" He laughs.

"Um . . . not exactly," I say. Our professor Dan loads the PowerPoint for today's lecture: CSC108

Introduction to Computer Science. The slide projects on two screens at the front of the lecture hall. The chitchat quiets to a murmur. "But that's over now. I'm in university."

Day 5: 9:00PM

I stare out the jail-like window, through the grid-like pattern, to the parking-lot. It's empty like the North Building and my inbox. I wait for the red-light.

"Hey. You're in CSC104?" someone says behind me. "Hey, you." A hand touches my shoulder.

I flinch. "Huh?"

A young man spinning his car keys on his index finger stands beside me. He has a white T-shirt and a silver linked chain and a diamond-studded cross that dangles off it. His beard is scruffy. His jeans are ripped but few of the threads are torn. He removes his Armani glasses and wipes the lenses with the corner of his shirt. "Didn't mean to startle you." He places his glasses on again. He looks at me head to toe. He grins. "I asked if you're in CSC104." He leans against the door, blocking the one beside me.

I debate whether I should respond. The halls remain empty. "Yeah, I'm in that class."

I text my brother. "Where are you?"

I stare at the almost-empty lot. Still no red-light.

"What's a cute girl doing in computer science?"

he questions.

The last car in the lot drives off. "Getting a degree," I reply.

"Haha, I was gonna ask. I know I won't be able to make next week's lecture. I have a hockey game. Can I have your number so I can get the notes from you?" He unlocks his Samsung-something and opens the contacts app. Before I can answer, he hands me his phone.

"Um, I guess so," I say.

He scans the parking lot then eyes the red notification light on my phone. He looks outside. "You have a boyfriend?"

"Why do you ask?" I enter my first name and phone number; nothing else.

"Just asking. Who are you waiting for?" he asks.

"My family is picking me up."

"You sure? I could give you a ride if you want. I have a car." He grins.

My ringtone startles me. The default sound is an alarm loud enough to wake you even at 6:00 AM. I hesitate. It's not a number I recognize.

"That's me. I wanted to make sure you gave me the right number," he says. "You sure you don't want a ride? I don't mind driving you, *at all*."

Saikiran pulls up in Nana's old car, the champagne coloured Infinity. "No thanks," I say. Saikiran's Adidas snap-back is a silhouette behind the tinted windows. I push my weight against the panic bar to exit North Building. The breeze makes the door heavy to open. Saikiran unlocks the car doors and I get in. I fasten my seatbelt before I press the home button. The red-light blinks. I leave it locked.

Day 17: Almost 9:00AM

My seat from day one, the seats beside it, ahead of it, and behind it, are taken. Daron's crew stole my spot. Lecture hall IB 120 has twenty-two other empty rows, so I look for a more hidden spot. I climb to the top, four rows from the back. I take a seat three chairs in. I have a great view of the classroom's dynamics. I slide back in my seat. I make myself as small, invisible, and silent as possible. A boy checks his iPhone as he enters the lecture hall. He rolls the sleeves of his dress shirt around the cuffs of his cardigan. He pauses, locks his iPhone, sips his Second Cup coffee, and glances around the room.

From up here, you can study compu-sci cliques. Here's what I see: to my left—empty. To my right—sparsely distributed trios, the kids who probably aren't in this program. Ahead of me—a few other asocial people, like myself. Front right: the passion-project coders, the ones who are fluent in English, Python, PHP, Java, C++, and probably only test their code once to find no errors. Front and centre—the coder boys who chat online but not in person. They type and click frantically, alternating between twelve open tabs, three open windows, two online role playing games, and lecture slides, just in case.

The hipster boy walks towards my row. I'm unsure if I've seen the khakis and hair grease before or if they're a common characteristic on this campus. We make eye contact. I avert my eyes and slide down in my seat. He looks around at the empty seats in this half of the lecture hall. I hope he chooses another row to sit in.

"Hey, you were at orientation, right?" he asks stopping beside me.

"Ya," I say.

"I remember you from the computer science info session. You always sit alone?" He takes the seat beside me. He uses another seat for his Hershel backpack.

He smells like eggs.

I hate eggs.

Day 19: 1:00PM

I roam through campus after class, following the flow. I float through IB, then the library, pass a group of Bible-pushers, and decline their goods with a polite, "No thank you." Posters across campus advertise some of the services offered at UTM. Some advertise the Walk Safer program for students who may feel unsafe on campus. Some remind students to "Wear a condom every time." Health and Counselling has free condoms available for students in need. Some inform us that there's Zumba every Monday and Wednesday in the dance studio.

The janitors smile as they pass us in the hallways as life sciences students put on their lab coats and lock up their belongings.

I return to the library. I follow the stairs to the basement. Eggman steps out of the computer lab. I pretend not to see him and swerve to find a seat in silent study.

"Sujaya," Eggman says behind me, "why do you always run away when you see me?"

I scan the bookshelves as if the titles have an answer.

"I don't. But I have to go now," I say. I search for the nearest exit. "Bye." I ditch the library and look for a hidden place to study. I move with the crowd again to Davis. I walk down the Recreational Athletics and Wellness Centre, the RAWC, staircase. The track and treadmills are busy, there's badminton in Gym A/B, and the pool windows are blocked off for Women's Only Hour. I look for a hidden area in the basement of Davis instead. The old lockers, flickering lights, and dirt, might explain the empty halls. I occupy a space in the furthest crevice of Davis. The room number was unbolted and left a faded teal rectangle against the grimy paint. I hope no one finds me.

Day 43: 8:00PM

I sit in silent study Googling methods of proving whether a number is prime or not. I alternate between tabs. I'm still stuck on the first day of MAT102: *Introduction to Mathematical Proofs.*

The red light is back: "When we gonna meet up?" It's Chris again.

"For what?" I respond. I wish one of these search results explained fields and axioms in conversational terms. I wish another tab explained why boys are odd creatures. I haven't recovered from the first lecture. The textbook resembles a novel, but it's words *and* numbers. It's a non-fiction horror story.

"So I can see you."

"Do you need help with the assignment or something?"

"Yeah, I'm completely lost . . . and I want to see you."

"I don't know how I can help you."

"That's why I need your help. Can we meet up? I thought I saw you in the library."

I close my laptop and pack my books. I tiptoe up from the basement and out of the library. I hope I make it to the Davis building unnoticed.

"`I can't help you,`" I respond.

"`Come on. This won't be your average study sesh. It'll be more interactive and engaging,`" he responds with a winky face.

I find my way back to the dusty corner in Davis. I use my sweater as a mat, spread out my laptop, notes, and pens, and try to refocus. Doors creak, lockers slam, and footsteps echo. I jump at every sound. I put headphones in and listen to silence. In my notebook, I write out prime numbers from one to one hundred. I wish this algorithm was as simple as writing: if number = prime: print ('true'). The Wiki page on prime numbers looks like an essay with embedded citations, but ordered lists are inserted where years should go. When I run my code, it results in twenty-seven errors. I don't know what I'm doing. I don't know where to find help.

Day 47: 11:00AM

Nine AM classes are university's version of penance. Class ends with another iClicker quiz on lists. Someone picks D even though it's still not an option. Dan reminds us that our upcoming assignment requires us to shuffle, but not the dance kind of shuffle, the code kind of shuffle. Shuffling seems like an easy concept until you're required to code it for the first time.

Daron swings the door open with enough momentum for him to pass through before it closes in my face. I hold the door open for the couple behind me. Daron stands outside the lecture hall and leans beside the class schedule. "You should study with us," Daron says. "We're going through calc."

Students pour out of IB and flood the library. Daron's buddies head out of IB and head towards the Hazel McCallion Academic Centre. Students sit at computer tables across the main floor. They log into the desktops but work on their laptops instead. Others cue playlists on YouTube. Some chug Red Bull desperately holding onto their focus. Some scroll through their Facebook feeds reading through the latest Spotted at UTM posts: UTM's anonymous gossip forum. One of Daron's friends looks back and grins at Daron as he passes through the double doors. Daron's buddy has the grey UofT hoodie that everyone on campus owns.

"Thanks for the invite, but I study better alone," I respond. The lineup at Second Cup is long. I'd join it to detour from this interaction. I usually run home between classes, but he caught me today.

"You might get better marks if you study with the guys though."

We exit IB. Starbucks by the library looks like a safe haven. "I'll be alright, but thank you for letting me know." I hold the door open for Daron as we enter the Hazel McCallion Academic Centre. Across from the library, people line up to order drinks and to pick up their drink orders. People chitchat and read from their MacBooks inside the café.

"How are you doing in calc anyways?" Daron asks. His buddies stand at the library entrance watching us talk. Daron's buddies point up to the third floor. They smile at Daron as if in admiration. When I make eye contact with them the smiles disintegrate and their gaze falls through the floor.

"I'm surviving," I say.

Daron nods at them, no longer invested in the conversation. "Yeah, it's light," he says, walking ahead. His friends mouth "You the man." I pretend not to notice. I pretend not to notice them staring. I pretend not to notice them fist-bump either.

"See ya," I say. He glances back just as his buddies congratulate him on his walk over. They distract him as I creep into Starbucks.

Day 53: 3:00PM

I stand among the crowd of caffeine-thirsting students in front of Tim Hortons. I feel bad for the servers. They run between the cash register and the Iced-Capp machine, frantically filling orders. They seem overwhelmed by the group of us demanding double-doubles.

"Sujaya," Daron says nudging my arm.

"Oh, hi." I smile back at him but turn to face the register.

He joins the line. "Didn't see you at the last group study session. You should've came."

The crowd grows but the line hasn't moved. Tim Hortons servers hand students red coffee cups and toasted bagels with cream cheese. Sometimes I like to think I'm like a honey crueller in a chocolate dipped world: always the odd one out. "I met with a different group," I say, still facing the register.

"You never come," he says behind me. "How'd you do on the last quiz?" One of the servers spills coffee on the counter and piles napkins over the mess.

"Not great," I respond. Another server takes over the register as the first server wipes up coffee. I'm next in line.

Daron scoffs. "I got a ninety on that. It was soft."

"Nice." I order my small double-double, pay with the Tim-Card Mom gave me, and stand beside the counter.

"You can still come and study with us. The guys think you're cool."

I fake laugh. "That's okay," I respond. The new server hands me my coffee.

"They were all asking me who the cute girl I was talking to was."

"Oh." I grab a sleeve from beside the register.

"They'll leave you alone if you come." He says. "Don't worry." He smiles.

Yesterday, Dad gave me advice: *sometimes you*

have to be mean.

"I'm just heading out now," I say, putting my Tim-Card back in my U-Pass holder.

Daron orders a plain bagel toasted with butter. I put in headphones and zip up my jacket. "Where are you going?" he asks.

"Heading out," I reply.

"Wait. You're leaving?" His smile disappears.

"I just want my space," I snap.

His expression frosts like the outside of an iced-capp. "Your loss, Sujaya."

CHAPTER 8: LAUNDRY

*I'll relax once queen sized beds are bigger
than king sized beds.*

I'm not arguing with you. It's a simple question," I say. I stand at Mom and Dad's bedroom door. The blinds are shut and the velvet curtains hide the remaining daylight. Dad lays silent on his half of the bed, wrapped in a blanket burrito. The other half of the bed is covered in a pile of Dad's, Saikiran's, and Mom's clean laundry. Mom pairs socks and tucks them in her top drawer.

The bedframe squeaks as Dad adjusts his position on the bed with his eyes still closed. "I have nothing to say," he answers.

I look at Mom. She folds a pile of Saikiran's Ninja Turtle T-shirts.

"I'm not here to argue about this. I'm just asking you what the difference is between a son and a daughter. Why can he go to a friend's house when I can't? I'm nineteen."

"I don't know these people. I don't know where you're going and who you're going with. I don't know what you're doing." Dad says. "End of story."

His eyes still closed.

I look at Mom hoping she'll back me up. Instead, she folds Saikiran's cargo pants. "You don't know my friends?" I ask. "The ones who came to our house? The ones I've known since grade one? The ones I won awards with?"

Mom stacks Saikiran's clothes. The bedframe creaks again as Dad shifts his weight. "No," he says. "I don't know these people."

Mom glances at me then looks back at the depleting pile of laundry.

"You never ask. That's not my fault. What's the difference between me and Saikiran then? Do you know Saikiran's friends?"

"He's always with the same boys," Dad says.

"You have a problem with my friends?" I ask. "Do I have to introduce each friend to you?"

"I don't want to talk about this," Dad says.

"It's not a new friend. It's Jennifer. You know her from Sawmill Valley."

Mom glares at me.

"End of discussion," Dad says.

"No. We're talking about this," I say. "I'm old enough to be in university and have a job. You know I'm old enough to gct married, right? But not old enough to go to my best friend's house and bake a cake? Mom, does this make any sense?"

Mom pairs socks.

"Saikiran can go out later in the day, to his

friend's house, do what he wants without question, and that's fine." I scoff. "Meanwhile, all he does during the day is watch TV. Does he even study?"

Mom and Dad are silent. Dad readjusts his position. "Don't argue with me," Dad says.

"Am I arguing?" I ask lowering my voice.

Mom doesn't respond. Her face is flushed. She folds pants from the laundry pile.

"I know, I'm the bad child. But, you say, if I don't know, ask. Now I'm asking."

Mom stops folding her work pants and looks at me with drained eyes. She shakes her head subtly, cautioning me.

"Why is it so hard to answer?" I ask. "Between two parents, neither can answer?"

Dad lays on the bed as if he's asleep. He's not snoring. He can hear me.

"One day I'll be out of here. I shouldn't have to suffocate in this house," I say.

Mom tucks Dad's work pants into his drawer. Dad cozies up in his blanket burrito and continues to fake sleep. I leave the room and swing their bedroom door closed behind me. I text Jennifer. "I hate being a brown girl sometimes."

*

Today's laundry day, the day I wash, fold, and put away the clothes mountain. I don't permit anyone to touch my clothes. On laundry day, I put each item back in its specific location. I hang my shirts in order of sleeve-length and colour. Patterned shirts have their own sections. I need a bigger laundry basket than the one in my room because this mountain of clothes has accumulated for at least two weeks.

Mom observes me as I walk down the stairs. I pretend she's invisible. Dad sits by the fish tank, watching our koi fish Lucky swim around, like he does every day. Saikiran watches highlights from the latest Barca game, flipping between Modern Family and CP24 to see the score of the Toronto FC game. Mom cleans out the fridge, emptying out last week's pelau and Shepherd's pie. The bottom stairs creak with my weight on them. Saikiran turns around on the couch and gives me his biggest grin.

"Oh, she's mad," he jokes.

Dad laughs along. "Come watch TV," Dad says. "Did you eat?"

I ignore them. I walk down to the basement, find a suitcase, and take it up to the main floor.

By now, Dad's feeding Lucky. Mom and Saikiran are folding wontons on the dining table. They all look equally confused. I drag the red suitcase, twice my size, to my room and lock the door. I take my laundry basket and dump the heap of dirty shirts and pants in it. Mom knocks on my door. I ignore it.

I take clean pairs of jeans and socks. I change my clothes. I lug the suitcase downstairs. Dad's seated in the living room watching the news on CP24. Tomorrow's high is twenty-four degrees. Mom stands by the stove frying wontons. Saikiran folds paper towels to absorb excess oil.

The suitcase makes a thud against the tiles as I pull it over the last step. Mom and Saikiran peer through the kitchen. Mom looks at my clothes and the suitcase, puzzled. Saikiran's playful grin fades.

Dad turns. I sit at the bottom step pretending to fix my socks. I re-zip the suitcase just for shits. "Hey. Where you going?" Dad asks. He lowers the volume of the TV. I raise the handle of the suitcase.

I roll the suitcase towards him and towards the basement. "Just doing laundry."

CHAPTER 9: HIDDEN INK

Not trying to be like anyone else,
not trying to be different either,
I just am.

I giggle like a child that just found the guitar they wished for under the Christmas tree. Aside from Jennifer and I, no one else knows.

"I thought I would cry." I say. I block all thoughts of explaining this to Mom. I'll tell her later.

"I told you it wasn't going to hurt!" Jennifer laughs. We thank our friendly tattoo artist and the lovely receptionist who fit us in today, exit Skintricate, and head back into Streetsville.

I fasten the button at the end of my left sleeve covering the bandage on my wrist. As we head towards Burrito Boyz across the street, I process what we did. Jennifer and I lied. Jennifer and I are supposed to be studying. This isn't permanent marker. *Blink.*

Over the next two days our friends notice our tattoos. They ask us all kinds of questions: "What does it mean? Did it hurt? Can I touch it? *Does your mom know?*"

I show them the lotus, in black ink, under the

palm of my left wrist. The lotus is strategically placed to hide at jobs and family events. I always, always, wear a watch.

I take the evening away from studying to watch The Big Bang Theory. I steal the remote and take Saikiran's spot on the couch. Sometimes, the brain-numbing effect of comedy helps me relax. Mom joins me in the living room with a folded piece of paper in her hand. The plan was to intro-duce her to the tattoo after the scab disappeared.

Okay, new plan.

She unfolds the receipt from Skintricate. "When were you going to show me?" She reads it over and points at the word *tattoo*. I probably shouldn't have hidden the receipt in my sock drawer. Her voice is calm, her expression is blank. She doesn't smile, but she doesn't frown.

I clear my throat. "After it healed."

She breaks her gaze. "Where is it?" She looks at my hands, at the receipt, and back to my hands. The sleeves of my robe cover my wrists.

I roll my sleeve to show the hidden ink on my wrist.

"Ah." Mom looks like she's staring at a dead rat.

"You don't like it?" I ask, stifling my laugh.

"Why would you do that?" Mom inhales a sharp breath. She re-reads the receipt. She says nothing.

The outline of the lotus is raised above the rest of my skin. The lotus has a dried black scab over it.

"It'll be healed in a few days," I reassure her.

The stairs creak as Dad's slippers hit against each step. I take the receipt from Mom's hand and hide it in my pocket. Mom mouths "Are you going to tell him?" I shake my head and raise the volume. I adjust my position on the couch to face the TV. Raj complains about his inability to speak to women while sober.

Dad hits the last two steps, I turn and whisper to Mom, "Don't worry. Nani has a tattoo."

CHAPTER 10: EGGS

*Twenty-one and more bitter
than the Angostura essence.*

T ell her what happened," Mom says. Dr. Isa closes the door with one hand, clipboard in the other. I wonder how she survives working eight hour days in heels. Mom's empty stare says she won't explain this one for me. Dr. Isa loads my patient profile on her computer. She crosses her toned legs as she reads through my history.

"So, you got dizzy?" Dr. Isa asks.

I wait for Mom to answer. Mom waits for me to answer.

"I was in a fitness class," I start, "and near the end I got dizzy." I look at Mom again. "I left the class. But I couldn't see," I say, my voice fades.

"Had you eaten anything that morning?"

"She doesn't eat," Mom murmurs.

"I had a salad for lunch," I answer.

"You don't eat breakfast?" Dr. Isa asks.

"I got up late," I lie.

Dr. Isa carefully types quickly with her long

nails. A box of extra-small examination gloves sits on her desk.

Mom inhales a sharp breath. "She hardly eats, but if she does eat, she'll only eat salad."

Dr. Isa looks at me and waits for an answer. I stay silent.

"Ask her," Mom says, she nods in my direction.

Dr. Isa looks at her computer screen. "Are you a vegetarian?"

"Yes."

"Do you eat eggs?"

"She hates eggs," Mom answers.

"Do you take B12 and iron?"

"I gave her an iron tablet yesterday," Mom answers.

"So that's all you've taken? Just the one?"

"Yes."

Dr. Isa rips a long sheet of examination table paper and sets it down. "Can you sit up here for me?" she asks. I climb onto the examination table. Dr. Isa shines a light in my eyes, then steps over to her desk and types something in her computer. She puts gloves on, and then uses a tongue depressor and a flashlight to examine inside my mouth. "Do you have a sore throat?"

I shrug. "I don't know," I say. It's felt weird for a few weeks now.

"It's red, and it looks sore – you must be used to it – so you can't really tell."

After she checks my weight, height, and reflexes with a rubber hammer, she types into her computer again. "Did you have other episodes of dizziness? When did it start?"

"It's happened a few times in the last two months," I pause, "but this was the first time everything went black."

"Have you lost a lot of weight recently?" she asks.

"No," I say.

Mom nods.

Dr. Isa types into her computer.

"Did you do anything out of the ordinary this time? Did you drink coffee? At the gym are you working out harder than you usually do?"

"No," I lie.

"This is common with teenage girls. Every one of them wants to be skinny. These Chatelaine magazines advertise these anorexic models. Let me tell you something, Sujaya. Your current weight is perfect for your age. You have absolutely nothing, nothing, wrong with you, and absolutely no weight to lose now. You have to stop this before you hurt yourself."

My eyes sting. I nod.

"If this is the case, here's what I'll tell you," she says. "It looks like you're dehydrated from working out too much. Your heart-rate is high. Your heart is beating fast because of the dehydration. You're not eating, or not eating enough, so your body is looking for nutrients that aren't there," she explains.

Mom says "See?" with her eyes.

"You're vegetarian, which is another factor, because you don't like eggs. That's an important food for you to eat. You're not getting enough protein, B12, and iron in the first place. When you stop eating your body looks for these things. You need starch, salt, and sugar. That's not what you get in a leafy salad. Salad is rabbit food." Dr. Isa sips her green tea as she looks over her computer screen. "Because you're vegetarian, and since you haven't been eating properly, I think there's a chance that anemia is contributing to the dizziness and passing out. The blood work will tell us that by Monday. Come in tomorrow and get that done." She prints out a blood test request form and hands it to me.

I nod.

"I want you to take iron every day. Drink Gatorade, or something with electrolytes, and eat. Your energy will only improve if you eat. That's most important. Salad is rabbit food. You need real food. *Starving isn't sexy.*"

Mom nods at me.

I clear my throat. "Okay," I agree.

Dr. Isa asks Mom to fill out some paperwork. She walks me over to the waiting room area. She returns to Mom at the reception desk and they talk. Mom nods as Dr. Isa explains something. The receptionist hands Mom my drivers license and health card. Dr. Isa's face remains cool, but Mom's serious. Mom and Dr. Isa murmur. "I'll do that," Mom says.

*

I fast. This time I fast for my blood test, but I have no appetite. I'm indifferent. At 10:00 AM, tubes of blood are drawn. By 10:20 AM my skin loses colour. In the waiting room window reflection, my face is pale. Dr. Isa tells Mom to take me for breakfast, and to make sure I eat something with egg in it. We pick up egg sandwiches and poutine from Burger King before Mom drops me to school. Mom already packed an enormous lunch for me: fruit, granola bars, juice, water, Gatorade, and a veggie burger.

"Eat the egg. I know you like poutine, so if you eat the egg you can take that with you," Mom says.

"This is too much food. I'm already full," I say.

"Well, you're not allowed to be hungry. Eat it."

We sit at a two-seater table at the back of Burger King. As Mom bites into her sandwich, she watches me as I have an internal crisis with the egg between the layered bread slices in my hands.

The bruise on my arm, where blood was extracted from, is green and purple. The soreness makes it difficult to raise my arm. The greasy, spongy texture of the egg has no appeal.

"We're not leaving here until you eat," Mom says.

"I have school."

Mom pushes the egg sandwich towards me. "Then eat."

I unwrap the sandwich. I take the little ketchup cup and dump it between the egg and the croissant. Mom crumples her wrapper and stares past me. She watches the cars lined up at the drive-through stop to order and to pick up. My stomach feels heavy and I feel nauseated. For once my stomach doesn't feel hollow. I crumple my wrapper.

Mom smiles when I put the empty wrapper on the plastic tray. "I'm happy when I see you eat," she says.

CHAPTER 11: STICKY NOTES PART I

Write it.

Nani is a Maharani, a queen, Nana calls her. She's always adorned with hand-crafted gold jewelry from India and Trinidad. Her midnight hair curls naturally, effortlessly. Nani wears bangles that clink as she slices green plums and seasons them with salt, lime juice, and enough pepper from the Trinidad market.

Nana's a Maharajah, a king. A diamond accented gold ring with a scorpion carved into it decorates his right hand. His white hair is meticulously combed back. He keeps a small brown comb in the front pocket of his shirt along with pens and knick-knacks for him to share.

Nana and I sit on the small couch by the TV, watching CP24, like we do every Friday when Saikiran and I get back from school. The weather forecast changes between this week's high of twenty and next week's high of twenty-four with a mix of sun and clouds.

Nana takes a pad of sticky notes from his pocket. He draws two almond eyes, round lips, and a pointed nose. The he draws long, wavy, blue hair, an arrow and writes "JAYA." When he finishes his drawing, Nana gives me his Parker Pen. I'll add it to the collection of Nana-pens in my pencil case. Nana hands me his bunch of keys and points at a small Ganesha keychain.

"Like it?" Nana asks.

"That's a cute Ganesha," I say. The keychain is a single tusked, half-man, half-elephant figure. This Ganesha holds a teeny tray of tiny laddoos. Ganesha's belly is round like Nana's.

Nana pulls another identical keychain from his pocket. He cups it in my hand.

"Weeey dem hands like ice! Let me see." Nana takes my hand and squeezes my fingers. Nana heats my frozen hands with his warm hands, twice the size of mine.

"My, you have such skinny little fingers. Go eat." He nods towards the dinner table.

"I just ate. I'm so full."

"You eat one piece ah roti an' yuh full? You doh eat nuhting?"

"I do eat. I had roti and soya," I say. I stretch and prolong my yawn. I hand Nana back his keys.

"I hear somebody's birthday is coming up," Nana says.

"I'm getting old. I don't like it," I joke.

Nani joins in. "You'll be seventeen just now, Jaya. I was seventeen when I got married." She tosses the salt, green plums, and seasoning in a bowl to make chow. We only get this kind of chow when Nani brings back green plums from the Trinidad market. "I was twelve when I met your Nana."

Mom sticks her head out from the kitchen. "That means you'll have to get married just now."

"Leave de gyal," Dad says.

Between channel flipping, Saikiran snickers.

"How many boyfrien' yuh have?" Nana asks.

"None," I say.

"It's okay, you can tell us," Mom says.

"She pretty. Plenty boys go like she," Nani says.

"She a smart gyal. You doh study no boy. You study school. Go to university. Boys go come laytah," Nana says.

"You haven't given me many options," I joke.

"Oooh," Saikiran says. "Okaaay then."

Lucky looks like he wants to jump out of the fish tank to eat the fish food in Dad's hand.

"Jaya," Nani says. "You know how I met Nana?"

"No," I answer.

"B, should I tell them the story?" B is Nani's pet name for Nana, short for Basdeo, but he goes by Vasudev, and I call him Nana.

Nana exhales a long breath, the most exasperated of sighs. "Go ahead, Tara."

"On my way to school on a Monday morning,

about three blocks away from my home, I used to pass by the variety store. In Trinidad, we call that a parlour. We used to buy a Penny-Cool at the parlour, it's like a Freezie. You need that when Trinidad gets hot-hot. A young boy owned it so there would always be a group of boys hanging out. We call that liming. This boy came for a week-long holiday and he came to me and asked me if there was any objection in talking to me. I replied yes. He went away. Lunch time I was going home for lunch, he came and asked me the same thing. Again, after school in the evening, he came to ask me. My answer was still yes. This went on 'till Wednesday and on Thursday I replied no.'"

Nani glances at Nana.

"Wow. He then walked with me to school and again he walked with me at lunch time. Well, well, well! Before I could reach home, three neighbours went to my home and told my mother how a boy was talking to me. They were so protective of me. When my mother asked me about the boy, I told her he only said good morning and good evening. He didn't stop talking to me and for the rest of the week he walked with me to and from school till Friday evening. He said we won't be able to see each other because he was leaving on Saturday to go back home. I lived in the North, in St. Augustine. He lived in Claxton Bay, way down south. Luckily for me, my sister sent me shopping and I had to go on that same route. So, I met him on that Saturday. As we were parting, he asked me for my address so he could write to me."

"Aww," I taunt, nudging Nana.

"Lucky for me I used to go to the post office after school to check if there was any mail. I was lucky to collect all the letters he sent to me. One day the post man started to deliver letters home. Wow!"

Nani drops her hands on the dining table. Her bangles chime.

I look at Mom. "No one sends me letters," I complain.

"No one writes letters now. You guys just text, it's easier," Mom responds.

"The only texts I get are from you and it's usually 'Wash the dishes,'" I say. We laugh. "Then what happened?" I ask Nani.

"When I got home, there was a letter for me which my mother received. My sister was patiently waiting for me. She was waiting to give me scary news. But mothers are so loving to their daughters," Nani smiles at Mom, "that when she asked me, I told her it must be the first time he did that. My mother believed me. I had to stop him from sending his letters to my home address."

"Did he stop sending letters?" I ask.

Nani shakes her head, laughing. "I asked my girlfriend for her address so he could send it to hers."

"Naughty Nani," I tease.

"She agreed but then one day her mom picked up a book and a letter fell from it. In those days, her mom couldn't read so she asked her daughter to read it to her. She found out it was mine. She then sent a message for me to meet her."

"Now you're in trouble," I tease.

"Before I went, I went in the school toilet, we called it the latrine, and I kneeled and prayed for Lord Jesus to help me."

Nana bursts in laughter.

"I was scared my father would stop me from going to school. My friend's mom made me promise not to do that anymore."

"You didn't stop, did you?"

"I did, but our love was so strong. I got another friend to have my letters sent to her address."

I gasp. "Bad girl," I say, pretending to scold her.

Nani smiles. "By this time, my father bought me a bicycle to ride because our school was one mile away. I used to walk that four times a day happily. But this friend lived another two miles away from school. After school, I would go whenever I thought there might be a letter. When I was almost fifteen years old, I got busy studying to become a teacher. Nana and I had no connection for a few months. But other boys hung out at the corner of the road where I lived. One day, one of the boys who was madly in love with me, sent me a request over the radio programme. Nana and his friends heard it and they got all excited. That triggered Nana to come and meet me. He was my boyfriend. It was a Saturday morning. They got in the car and came driving by my house. They were just lucky to see me as they drove by. As I was going to classes, he came to talk to me. I told him that my mother said if any boy liked me to tell that boy to meet her. When I told him that, he said okay."

I look at Nana. "You weren't scared?" I ask. He shrugs.

Nani continues, "I went to my classes, but when I got home I saw him on the roadside talking to my neighbour with my mother. Oh my god. I got scared."

Nana places his sticky note drawing of a monkey and rests it on my knee. "Nana's not scared of anything," I say, "except my cold hands."

"Nah, me eh scared," Nana says before I press my icy hands against his cheeks. "Chil' you made of ice or what?"

Nani clears her throat and continues with her story. "He was brave in telling my mother that he wanted to marry her daughter. My mother said she could not give him an answer and that he should talk to my father first. He came to the house and waited, but my father was late. My mother told him he would have to come back another day. He did not wait long."

"How long did he wait?" I ask.

"He came back the next day," Nani says. "It was Christmas time and we were cleaning the house and varnishing chairs and so on. He spoke to my father who told him that he would have to wait for five years. He replied, 'That's okay, I'll wait ten.' I wrote my first year of exams for teaching but he soon after told me that I had to stop school. His mother would not want his wife to work after we got married. I had to stop school. Then we got married."

"Ay," Nana says. He points his finger at me. "You doh study no boy." Nana hands me another pen. "School first."

CHAPTER 12: VANILLA

*You decide what changes you and
who you change with.*

Vijaisai is seventeen today. The lil' cuzzie is growing up. Around six, Mom, Saikiran, and I head over to Sathya, Sujana, and Vijaisai's house. Vijaisai answers the door. He has different shades of lipstick, like face paint, all over his cheeks. On the front mat, over the checkered tiles, shoes are scattered by the door: Lini Mami's heels, Nani's sandals, Sujana's sneakers and Adithya, Anand, and Agnesh's Pumas.

"Happy birthday lil bro," I say.

"Thanks Jaya," Vijaisai says. He's nearly six feet tall and hovers above me as I hug him. Mom hands Sathya a cooler bag with homemade bowtie pasta and sweet and sour soya.

"You're looking tiny, Jaya," Lini Mami says. Her Trini accent turns everything she says into a melody. She brushes the back of her hand against my cheek. No matter what I pick, all my clothes are baggy now. A black blouse and jeans seem safe, but I still need a belt to hold them up.

I smile. "You look young as always," I say.

Her fingers slip off my cheekbone as she finds no cheek left to pinch. "So pretty," she says light-heartedly. Lini Mami's slim, like she was when I ran around with Adithya, Anand, and Saikiran, making spidey-potions.

I laugh. "Thank you."

"Cehfull, dem boys go like yuh, eh?" Nani says in her Trini accent. She wears a ruby red embroidered blouse she had tailored for her in India. She wears her favorite long black skirt that flows over her broad hips. "Make sho yuh find a nice boy." Nani laughs as she carries aloo pie to the dining room. Aloo pie is one of Nani's famous appetisers. It has seasoned potatoes, mashed, wrapped in dough, and fried. Aloo pie is also what we call our youngest cousin, Agnesh.

A familiar aroma fills the house: Rupa Mami's homemade pizza. No one turns down Rupa Mami's pizza. Adithya, Anand, and Agnesh play chutney music in the living room. The kitchen tiles transform into Mom and Nani's dance floor while everyone hugs the birthday boy.

Dinner starts at 7:05. One table is set in the kitchen, another is set in the dining room. We say Brahmarpanam, a meal prayer, before we eat. Everyone dishes out their own food, buffet style. Traditional party foods line the island in the kitchen: macaroni pie, fried rice, chow mein, soya, wontons, homemade pizza, bowtie pasta, curry aloo (potato), sweet and sour soya, and roti.

I help myself to pizza, pasta, soya, roti, and wontons. It's not everything, but it fills my plate.

Almost ten years have passed and almost all the cousins maintained the same eating tactics we had as kids. Anand picks his onions out and pushes them aside. Sujana keeps her roti on a separate plate. Agnesh only fills up on pizza. Sathya enjoys his curry aloo and roti. Vijaisai and Saikiran organize their food. Nothing can touch.

Nani passes our table and inspects our plates. "Anand, you want more dhal-puri?" Anand nods. He takes a handful of the split-pea stuffed roti between bites. She looks at Saikiran's plate, Agnesh's plate, Sathya and Sujana's plates, then stops at mine. "Yuh try dee aloo?" she asks.

"Maybe later. I'm full," I say.

She laughs. "Okay, second rounds. You always full."

Sastri Mamu, Vijaisai's dad, and Mom's eldest brother, checks up on us. "How's Jaya-ka-shmaya?" he asks. He never explained how he came up with that nickname, but it stuck.

Everyone cracks up. "I'm good," I say. Sastri Mamu ruffles my hair.

"You taking your iron, Jaya?" he asks.

"Um . . . sometimes," I say. "It hurts my stomach."

"Try to take it after you eat," he says. "Okay?"

I nod.

After dinner, the tables are cleared. We seat Vijaisai in the centre of the kitchen table. Candles are lit, "Happy Birthday" is sung, and Vijaisai fans out the candles with his hand because he does not want to "spit on the cake".

Rupa Mami passes out slices of frosted vanilla cake, with vanilla custard, and vanilla ice cream on the side. She grins as she hands me the chocolate-free dessert. She knows I don't like chocolate.

Vijaisai opens his gifts: money and money, soccer tickets and money, an Apple watch and money. It's a sweet seventeen for him.

Later in the evening, Adithya, Anand, and Agnesh set up something on the big screen T.V. in the living room. Home videos from 2005. I forgot we made home videos, mortifying videos.

"Let's go home," I tell Mom. Her back is turned and she doesn't hear me.

"You have to see Jaya in this one," Adithya says, laughing.

"If you put that on, I'm going home," I say.

"No, come on, you look so cute in it. We all do. Come on Jaya," Anand says. Anand puts his hand on my shoulder.

I fling it off. "No. I'm leaving. I don't want to see that." My voice is cold.

"You were so cute in those videos, I should pinch you," Rupa Mami says. In the past ten years, she too hasn't changed. The only difference now is the strands of gold she added to her hair. She reaches for my face.

I flinch.

I clear my throat. "I'm not watching it. I'm going in the other room." My face feels hot.

Rupa Mami frowns. "Okay guys, Jaya doesn't want to watch it, put on something else," she says. The blue screen on the TV flickers. We see a short, round-faced, ten-year-old, me.

I stare at the ten-year-old version of myself. I hold my breath. My throat burns. I walk away from the living room. I walk away from Nani and the rest of the family. I sit on a couch alone in the front room of the house. I take slow breaths and blink until my eyes stop tearing up. The family continues to laugh and comment on how small we all were.

"Jaya!" Vadie Mamu calls.

"What is *that*?" Agnesh says as he laughs.

"Jaya! Look how cute you are! Come!" Lini Mami says.

Sathya walks into the front room where I am, smiling. "Come see! You're so cute!"

"I don't want to watch it," I say. I try to clear my throat. He holds my arm and makes a playful pull for me to get up.

"Come Jaya, everybody's waiting for you."

"I don't want to see it," I say. My voice cracks. I look down at the torn leather on the arm rest.

Sathya freezes. "What? Why are you crying? What's wrong?"

"I don't want to see it," I repeat.

"You want to be alone?" he asks.

I nod. Tears stream down my cheeks onto my shirt. Sujana peeks into the room, but shuffles back to the living room where my family bonds over memories of our childhood. A minute later, Rupa Mami scurries towards me from the living room. I dab the corners of my eyes with the edge of my sleeve. My runny mascara stains it like calligraphy ink.

"Oh, Jaya, what happened?" Rupa Mami asks. She squats before the couch and cradles my face in her hands.

"I didn't want to watch it," I say between sobs.

Sujana joins us in the living room; Lini Mami walks in at the same time. Sujana is seven years older than me and petite, like me.

"Sujana can you get Jaya some tissues?" Rupa Mami asks. Sujana nods.

"Why didn't you want to watch it?" she asks.

I shake my head.

"Because they made fun of you?"

I shake my head.

"You don't like the way you looked?"

I nod. I cover my face. Sujana hands me a tissue and passes her hand over my hair again and again.

"You look so cute in the video, Jaya," Sujana

says.

I gaze at the arm rest to avoid looking her in the eye.

"I've never seen you like this before. You've never cried before. You know those Barbie dolls from India? The Bharat Nathyam dance dolls? That's what you looked like to me," Rupa Mami says kneeling on the floor.

"No." Hot tears roll down my cheeks. "I was so fat," I say. Mom sits on the couch across from me. In her ruffled top and petite dress pants. She stares at me looking for an answer. I sniffle and pull a tissue from the box in my lap.

"Oh my God. You were never fat, Jaya," Lini Mami says. I pull another tissue. It's the expensive brand. It's soft.

"You were such a pretty girl then, and look at how nice you are now. Like, *wow*," Lini Mami says.

"She's too nice." Mom's voice cracks. Tears flow down her rosy cheeks.

Rupa Mami turns to Mom. "Oh! Why are you crying now, too?"

Mom's breath is staggered as she speaks. "It's so hard to know what's going on with her. She never says anything is wrong, when it is. She never acts like anything is wrong, and then she . . ." Mom wipes her eyes with the back of her hand. "I never know."

My words break as I speak. "I just know how

hard it was to stop looking like that. I don't like remembering that."

"Look at you," Lini Mami says. "Adithya had the same problem growing up and he still does now. At school they would call him names, and he would get upset. At the gym, one of the guys he used to work out with said, "Man you got so fat!" Before, this guy was his friend. At first he would get upset and fight with those people. But now you know what? He knows what he is. He knows that he works out, but there is nothing wrong with him. So if those guys want to make fun, he says 'So what? That's how I am', because they can't say that he doesn't try."

"That's true," I say.

"At school, Vijaisai still gets picked on all the time. He knows who he is and that there is nothing wrong with the way he is. Being bigger is not a bad thing. It doesn't change you." Rupa Mami continues, "I was chubby too when I was small. I only slimmed down after I started playing sports. They used to make fun of me. But it was just fat, it doesn't change you." Rupa Mami sits right next to me. "There's nothing wrong with you. There was nothing wrong with you. Look at you," she gestures towards me with her hand, up and down. "You were perfect then. You're perfect now." Rupa Mami gives me a hug before she stands up and walks back to the living room.

I grip the wad of tissues in my hand.

"Your cousins were just joking with you, Jaya. None of us knew this bugged you so much," Lini Mami says.

"It's okay," I say.

Rupa Mami reappears. "They skipped the parts you were in, okay?"

I smile.

"You good now?" Mom asks.

"Better."

The birthday boy, Adithya, Anand, Agnesh, and Saikiran walk over. "We skipped the parts you were in, Jaya, don't worry," Agnesh says. Agnesh is the only cousin born after the nineties. He's taller than me too.

"Thanks guys," I say.

"Wanna watch it with us? You can see Dit dressed like a monkey," Agnesh says.

"Who you calling Dit, Aloo?" Adithya replies.

I stand up and push Adithya and Agnesh towards the living room. "Let's go."

Anand rests his chin on my head as he pulls me into a hug. "You good, Jaya?"

"I'm good."

To my family,

For music lessons,
Kumon,
Balvikas class,
road trips,
rebuttals,
and encouragement,
thank you.

sujaya

name | su-jay-a| / 'sue-jay-uh'/

def. victory or triumph

Epilogue: Sticky Notes Part II

Positivity is a full-time job. You don't get paid,
but it pays off.

Nani's footsteps sound from the bottom of the staircase. Nani always checks up on me. She worries when I'm stressed. Today she brought comfort food: stew soya-chicken, because *grandmothers know*.

I'm a bad granddaughter. I never call. I hate talking on the phone, but that's no excuse. I should make time. I know I should check up on Nani more often now that Nana's gone. Mom stays with Nani during the week. Dad and Saikiran alternate which days they drop me to school. Saikiran and I usually stay with Nani on weekends.

I peer outside my bedroom door. Nani fidgets with a small stack of sticky notes between her fingers as she enters my bedroom.

"Jaya, tell me again what you study? I tried to explain it to Aunty Savy but me eh know what it is."

I laugh. "No one knows what CCT is, not even me," I say. "There's no easy way to explain it. I study communications, culture, and information technology. That's one major. I have a second major in professional writing and communications."

Nani blinks.

"One day I'm working on a video, and the next an essay, or a web site, or a story, or taking photos. I'm in communications and it's still hard to explain."

"That's why you have to go to UTM and Sheridan?" she asks.

"Yeah," I say.

"And why you're so busy?" Nani asks.

"When I'm not busy, I feel useless. So, I think this kind of stress is good stress."

"So, tell me again about this project," she says. Nani pulls the desk chair and takes a seat.

I shuffle through printed copies of stories I wrote in second year. The "cringe pile," I call it. I shift the memory clutter away from Nani and take a seat at my desk—my bed. "I'm collecting stories for a writing class," I say. "That's why I asked you to tell me how you met Nana again."

Nani flips through the pages before she hands me the stack of stickies. The small square notepad is covered in her cursive handwriting. Each yellow sticky is numbered from one to eighteen. The words *boyfriend* and *wow* are triple-underlined and bolded.

"I was just sitting down doing nothing and I thought, I better write it." She hands me a half-stylus, half-pen. White ink on the red barrel reads,

In loving memory of Sri Vasudev Maharajh.

WRITE HERE

Write now.

Write Here

WRITE HERE

WRITE HERE